McLoughlin

by Iain Gray

Lang**S**yne

PUBLISH

WRITING *to* REMEMBER

LangSyne

PUBLISHING

WRITING *to* REMEMBER

Strathclyde Business Centre
120 Carstairs Street, Glasgow G40 4JD
Tel: 0141 554 9944 Fax: 0141 554 9955
E-mail: info@scottish-memories.co.uk
www.langsyneshop.co.uk

Design by Dorothy Meikle
Printed by Hay Nisbet Press, Glasgow
© Lang Syne Publishers Ltd 2008

ISBN 1-85217-268-1

McLoughlin

MOTTO:
Remember your promises
(and) Brave and trusty.

CREST:
A triple-towered castle
atop a crest coronet.

NAME variations include:
MacLochlainn *(Gaelic)*,
Ó Máoilsheáchlainn *(Gaelic)*,
O Melaghlin *(Gaelic)*,
Lochlain, MacGloughlin,
McGloughin, MacLaughlin,
McLaughlin, MacLoughlin.

Chapter one:
Origins of Irish surnames

**According to an old saying, there are two types of Irish –
those who actually are Irish and those who wish they were.**

This sentiment is only one example of the allure that the
high romance and drama of the proud nation's history holds
for thousands of people scattered across the world today.

It's a sad fact, however, that the vast majority of Irish
surnames are found far beyond Irish shores, rather than on
the Emerald Isle itself.

The population stood at around eight million souls in
1841, but today it stands at fewer than six million.

This is mainly a tragic consequence of the potato
famine, also known as the Great Hunger, which devastated
Ireland between 1845 and 1849.

The Irish peasantry had become almost wholly reliant
for basic sustenance on the potato, first introduced from the
Americas in the seventeenth century.

When the crop was hit by a blight, at least 800,000
people starved to death while an estimated two million
others were forced to seek a new life far from their native
shores – particularly in America, Canada, and Australia.

The effects of the potato blight continued until about
1851, by which time a firm pattern of emigration had
become established.

Ireland's loss, however, was to the gain of the countries in which the immigrants settled, contributing enormously, as their descendants do today, to the well being of the nations in which their forefathers settled.

But those who were forced through dire circumstance to establish a new life in foreign parts never forgot their roots, or the proud heritage and traditions of the land that gave them birth.

Nor do their descendants.

It is a heritage that is inextricably bound up in the colourful variety of Irish names themselves – and the origin and history of these names forms an integral part of the vibrant drama that is the nation's history, one of both glorious fortune and tragic misfortune.

This history is well documented, and one of the most important and fascinating of the earliest sources are *The Annals of the Four Masters*, compiled between 1632 and 1636 by four friars at the Franciscan Monastery in County Donegal.

Compiled from earlier sources, and purporting to go back to the Biblical Deluge, much of the material takes in the mythological origins and history of Ireland and the Irish.

This includes tales of successive waves of invaders and settlers such as the Fomorians, the Partholonians, the Nemedians, the Fir Bolgs, the Tuatha De Danann, and the Laigain.

Of particular interest are the *Milesian Genealogies*,

because the majority of Irish clans today claim a descent from either Heremon, Ir, or Heber – three of the sons of Milesius, a king of what is now modern day Spain.

These sons invaded Ireland in the second millennium B.C, apparently in fulfilment of a mysterious prophecy received by their father.

This Milesian lineage is said to have ruled Ireland for nearly 3,000 years, until the island came under the sway of England's King Henry II in 1171 following what is known as the Cambro-Norman invasion.

This is an important date not only in Irish history in general, but for the effect the invasion subsequently had for Irish surnames.

'Cambro' comes from the Welsh, and 'Cambro-Norman' describes those Welsh knights of Norman origin who invaded Ireland.

But they were invaders who stayed, inter-marrying with the native Irish population and founding their own proud dynasties that bore Cambro-Norman names such as Archer, Barbour, Brannagh, Fitzgerald, Fitzgibbon, Fleming, Joyce, Plunkett, and Walsh – to name only a few.

These 'Cambro-Norman' surnames that still flourish throughout the world today form one of the three main categories in which Irish names can be placed – those of Gaelic-Irish, Cambro-Norman, and Anglo-Irish.

Previous to the Cambro-Norman invasion of the twelfth century, and throughout the earlier invasions and settlement of those wild bands of sea rovers known as the Vikings in the eighth and ninth centuries, the population of the island was relatively small, and it was normal for a person to be identified through the use of only a forename.

But as population gradually increased and there were many more people with the same forename, surnames were adopted to distinguish one person, or one community, from another.

Individuals identified themselves with their own particular tribe, or 'tuath', and this tribe – that also became known as a clann, or clan – took its name from some distinguished ancestor who had founded the clan.

The Gaelic-Irish form of the name Kelly, for example, is Ó Ceallaigh, or O'Kelly, indicating descent from an original 'Ceallaigh', with the 'O' denoting 'grandson of.' The name was later anglicised to Kelly.

The prefix 'Mac' or 'Mc', meanwhile, as with the clans of the Scottish Highlands, denotes 'son of.'

Although the Irish clans had much in common with their Scottish counterparts, one important difference lies in what are known as 'septs', or branches, of the clan.

Septs of Scottish clans were groups who often bore an entirely different name from the clan name but were under the clan's protection.

In Ireland, septs were groups that shared the same name and who could be found scattered throughout the four provinces of Ulster, Leinster, Munster, and Connacht.

The 'golden age' of the Gaelic-Irish clans, infused as their veins were with the blood of Celts, pre-dates the Viking invasions of the eighth and ninth centuries and the Norman invasion of the twelfth century, and the sacred heart of the country was the Hill of Tara, near the River Boyne, in County Meath.

Known in Gaelic as 'Teamhar na Rí', or Hill of Kings, it was the royal seat of the 'Ard Rí Éireann', or High King of Ireland, to whom the petty kings, or chieftains, from the island's provinces were ultimately subordinate.

It was on the Hill of Tara, beside a stone pillar known as the Irish 'Lia Fáil', or Stone of Destiny, that the High Kings were inaugurated and, according to legend, this stone would emit a piercing screech that could be heard all over Ireland when touched by the hand of the rightful king.

The Hill of Tara is today one of the island's main tourist attractions.

Opposition to English rule over Ireland, established in the wake of the Cambro-Norman invasion, broke out frequently and the harsh solution adopted by the powerful forces of the Crown was to forcibly evict the native Irish from their lands.

These lands were then granted to Protestant colonists, or 'planters', from Britain.

Many of these colonists, ironically, came from Scotland and were the descendants of the original 'Scotti', or 'Scots', who gave their name to Scotland after migrating there in the fifth century A.D., from the north of Ireland.

Colonisation entailed harsh penal laws being imposed on the majority of the native Irish population, stripping them practically of all of their rights.

The Crown's main bastion in Ireland was Dublin and its environs, known as the Pale, and it was the dispossessed peasantry who lived outside this Pale, desperately striving to eke out a meagre living.

It was this that gave rise to the modern-day expression of someone or something being 'beyond the pale'.

Attempts were made to stamp out all aspects of the ancient Gaelic-Irish culture, to the extent that even to bear a Gaelic-Irish name was to invite discrimination.

This is why many Gaelic-Irish names were anglicised with, for example, and noted above, Ó Ceallaigh, or O'Kelly, being anglicised to Kelly.

Succeeding centuries have seen strong revivals of Gaelic-Irish consciousness, however, and this has led to many families reverting back to the original form of their name, while the language itself is frequently found on the fluent tongues of an estimated 90,000 to 145,000 of the island's population.

Ireland's turbulent history of religious and political strife is one that lasted well into the twentieth century, a landmark century that saw the partition of the island into the twenty-six counties of the independent Republic of

Ireland, or Eire, and the six counties of Northern Ireland, or Ulster.

Dublin, originally founded by Vikings, is now a vibrant and truly cosmopolitan city while the proud city of Belfast is one of the jewels in the crown of Ulster.

It was Saint Patrick who first brought the light of Christianity to Ireland in the fifth century A.D.

Interpretations of this Christian message have varied over the centuries, often leading to bitter sectarian conflict – but the many intricately sculpted Celtic Crosses found all over the island are symbolic of a unity that crosses the sectarian divide.

It is an image that fuses the 'old gods' of the Celts with Christianity.

All the signs from the early years of this new millennium indicate that sectarian strife may soon become a thing of the past – with the Irish and their many kinsfolk across the world, be they Protestant or Catholic, finding common purpose in the rich tapestry of their shared heritage.

Chapter two:
Myth and legend

**The McLoughlins of today and their various namesakes
such as the McLaughlins can lay claim to a proud
heritage rooted deeply in the ancient soil of Ireland.**

The name was originally the Gaelic Ó
Máoilscheáchlainn, or MacLochlainn, later appearing as
O'Melaghlin.

One theory is that the MacLochlainn form derived from
the personal name Lachlan, denoting 'heroic, or warrior-
like', while other sources assert the name has Norse origins,
first brought to Ireland in the eighth and ninth centuries A.D.
by Viking invaders.

There is evidence, however, that the name was already
in existence on the island before the Viking invasions and
settlements.

The Ó Máoilscheáchlainn form is said to denote
'descendant of Malachy', while other sources assert it
indicates 'follower of St. Secundius.'

The anglicised form McLoughlin/McLaughlin became
common in later centuries, with the 'ou' form found today
mainly near Dublin, in Connacht, Leinster, and the south of
the Republic, with the 'au' form more common in the north
of the island.

There were two important and separate septs of what

later became the McLoughlins/McLaughlins of today: these
were the McLoughlins of Ulster and, further south, the
McLoughlins of Meath.

There were also the McLoughlins of Galway who,
despite originally being known in Gaelic as 'Lochnaidh',
shared a common descent with the McLoughlins of Ulster
and the McLoughins of Meath.

This was from the celebrated Niall Noíghiallach, better
known to posterity as the great warrior king Niall of the
Nine Hostages.

The dramatic life and times of this ancestor of the
McLoughlins are steeped in stirring Celtic myth and legend.

The youngest son of Eochaidh Mugmedon, king of the
province of Connacht, his mother died in childbirth and he
was brought up by his evil stepmother Mongfhinn who, for
reasons best known to herself, was determined that he
should die.

She accordingly abandoned him naked on the Hill of
Tara, inauguration site of the Ard Rí, or High Kings, of
Ireland, but he was found by a wandering bard who took
him back to his father.

One legend is that Mongfhinn sent Niall and his four
brothers – Brian, Fiachra, Ailill, and Fergus – to a renowned
prophet who was also a blacksmith to determine which of
them would succeed their father as Ard Rí.

The blacksmith, known as Sitchin, set the lads a task by
deliberately setting fire to his forge.

Niall's brothers ran in and came out carrying the spear-heads, fuel, hammers, and barrels of beer that they had rescued, but Niall staggered out clutching the heavy anvil so vital to the blacksmith's trade.

By this deed, Sitchin prophesied that Niall would be the one who would take on the glorious mantle of kingship.

Another prophetic incident occurred one day while Niall and his brothers were engaged in the hunt.

Thirsty from their efforts they encountered an ugly old woman who offered them water – but only in return for a kiss.

Three of the lads, no doubt repelled by her green teeth and scaly skin, refused. Fiachra pecked her lightly on the cheek and, by this act, she prophesied that he would one day reign at Tara – but only briefly.

The bold Niall, however, kissed her fully on the lips. The hag then demanded that he should now have full sexual intercourse with her and, undaunted, he did so.

Through this action she was suddenly transformed into a stunningly beautiful young woman known as Flaithius, or Royalty, who predicted that he would become the greatest High King of Ireland.

His stepmother Mongfhinn later tried to poison him, but accidentally took the deadly potion herself and died.

This legend relates to what was known as the Festival of Mongfhinn, or Feis na Samhan (the Fest of Samhain), because it was on the evening of October 31, on Samhain's

Eve, that the poisoning incident is said to have taken place.

It was believed for centuries in Ireland that, on Samhain Eve, Mongfhinn's warped and wicked spirit would roam the land in hungry search of children's souls.

The Festival, or Feast, of Samhain, is today better known as Halloween.

Niall became Ard Rí in 379 A.D. and embarked on the series of military campaigns and other daring adventures that would subsequently earn him the title of Niall of the Nine Hostages.

The nine countries and territories into which he raided and took hostages for ransom were the provinces of Munster, Leinster, Connacht, and Ulster; Britain, and the territories of the Saxons, Morini, Picts, and Dalriads.

Niall's most famous hostage was a young lad known as Succat, son of Calpernius, a Romano-Briton who lived in the area of present day Milford Haven, on the Welsh coast.

Later known as Patricius, or Patrick, he became renowned as Ireland's patron saint, St. Patrick, responsible for bringing the light of Christianity to the island in the early years of the fifth century A.D.

Raiding in Gaul, in the area of Boulogne-sur-mer in present day France, Niall was ambushed and killed by one of his treacherous subjects in 405 A.D.

But his legacy survived in the form of his sons who founded branches of what was known as the Hy Niall or Uí Neill dynasties.

One son founded the northern Uí Neill dynasty, and one of the clans that was a member of this mighty clan confederation was the clan of the McLoughlins of Ulster.

The McLoughlins of the ancient kingdom of Meath were members of the southern Uí Neill, founded by another of Niall's sons, while the McLoughlins of Galway traced a descent from another son.

It was the McLoughlins of Ulster who also founded the great Scottish clan of MacLachlan, after a branch of the family settled in Argyllshire.

The McLoughlins/McLaughlins are in fact recognised to this day as a sept of Clan MacLachlan and accordingly entitled to share in its proud heritage and traditions, including motto, crest, and tartan.

Staunch supporters of the Royal House of Stuart, the MacLachlans were also at the forefront of Scotland's long and bloody struggle against England for freedom and independence, with a MacLachlan Chief recorded as a supporter of the great warrior king Robert the Bruce.

The 17th Chief of the clan was killed at the battle of Culloden in April of 1746 after leading his clansmen in the abortive cause of Charles Edward Stuart, better known as Bonnie Prince Charlie.

The namesake of the McLoughlins of Meath was Malachy, Ard Rí, or High King of Ireland from 844 to 860 A.D. while one of his successors was his son Flann Sionna, or Flann of the Shannon, who ruled from 876 to 941 A.D.

The power and influence of the McLoughlins steadily increased, through its association with the Uí Neill dynasty, but what ultimately proved to be the death knell of their way of life and that of many other native Irish clans was sounded in the late twelfth century in the form of foreign invasion – an invasion in which a McLoughlin chief played an unwitting part.

Chapter three:

Precious legacy

Twelfth century Ireland was far from being a unified nation, split up as it was into territories ruled over by squabbling chieftains who ruled as kings in their own right – and this inter-clan rivalry worked to the advantage of the invaders.

In a series of bloody conflicts one chieftain, or king, would occasionally gain the upper hand over his rivals, and by 1156 the most powerful was Muirchertach MacLochlainn, king of the powerful O'Neills and Ard Rí of Ireland.

He was opposed by the equally powerful Rory O'Connor, king of the province of Connacht, but he increased his power and influence by allying himself with Dermot MacMurrough, king of Leinster.

MacLochlainn and MacMurrough were aware that the main key to the kingdom of Ireland was the thriving trading port of Dublin that had been established by invading Vikings, or Ostmen, in 852 A.D.

The combined forces of MacLochlainn and MacMurrough took Dublin, but when MacLochlainn was killed in 1166 the Dubliners rose up in revolt and overthrew the unpopular MacMurrough.

A triumphant Rory O'Connor entered Dublin and was later inaugurated as Ard Rí, but MacMurrough refused to accept defeat.

He appealed for help from England's Henry II in unseating O'Connor, an act that was to radically affect the future course of Ireland's fortunes.

The English monarch agreed to help MacMurrough, but distanced himself from direct action by delegating his Norman subjects in Wales with the task.

These ambitious and battle-hardened barons and knights had first settled in Wales following the Norman Conquest of England in 1066 and, with an eye on rich booty, plunder, and lands, were only too eager to obey their sovereign's wishes and furnish MacMurrough with aid.

MacMurrough crossed the Irish Sea to Bristol, where he rallied powerful barons such as Robert Fitzstephen and Maurice Fitzgerald to his cause, along with Gilbert de Clare, Earl of Pembroke.

The mighty Norman war machine soon moved into action, and so fierce and disciplined was their onslaught on the forces of Rory O'Connor and his allies that by 1171 they had re-captured Dublin, in the name of MacMurrough, and other strategically important territories.

A nervous Henry II now began to take cold feet over the venture, realising that he may have created a rival in the form of a separate Norman kingdom in Ireland.

Accordingly, he landed on the island, near Waterford, at the head of a large army in October of 1171 with the aim of curbing the power of his Cambro-Norman barons.

Protracted war between the king and his barons was

averted, however, when they submitted to the royal will, promising homage and allegiance in return for holding the territories they had conquered in the king's name.

Henry also received the submission and homage of many of the Irish chieftains, tired as they were with internecine warfare and also perhaps realising that as long as they were rivals and not united they were no match for the powerful forces the English Crown could muster.

English dominion over Ireland was ratified through the Treaty of Windsor of 1175, under the terms of which Rory O'Connor, for example, was allowed to rule territory unoccupied by the Normans in the role of a vassal of the king.

Further waves of Anglo-Norman settlers descended on the island – at the expense of many native Irish clans such as the McLoughlins who were steadily pushed and dispersed from their ancient homelands.

Much of the McLoughlin territory in Meath, for example, was lost to the powerful Norman baron Hugh de Lacy, while more territory was lost through the English Crown's policy of settling, or 'planting' loyal Protestants on Irish land.

This policy had started during the reign from 1491 to 1547 of Henry VIII, whose Reformation effectively outlawed the established Roman Catholic faith throughout his dominions.

The settlement of loyal subjects of the Crown continued throughout the subsequent reigns of Elizabeth I, James I (James VI of Scotland), and Charles I.

Ireland groaned under a weight of oppression that was

directed in the main against native Irish clans such as the McLoughlins.

An indication of the harsh treatment meted out to them can be found in a desperate plea sent to Pope John XII by Roderick O'Carroll of Ely, Donald O'Neil of Ulster, and a number of other Irish chieftains in 1318.

They stated: 'As it very constantly happens, whenever an Englishman, by perfidy or craft, kills an Irishman, however noble, or however innocent, be he clergy or layman, there is no penalty or correction enforced against the person who may be guilty of such wicked murder.

'But rather the more eminent the person killed and the higher rank which he holds among his own people, so much more is the murderer honoured and rewarded by the English, and not merely by the people at large, but also by the religious and bishops of the English race.'

This appeal to the Pope had little effect on what became the increasingly harsh policy of the occupying English Crown against the native Irish – and the inevitable outcome was a series of rebellions.

In their rebellion against the Crown the McLoughlins joined forces with the ill-fated Sir Cahir O'Doherty.

A number of Irish earls had rebelled against the policy of plantation and penal policies against Catholics but, following their defeat at the battle of Kinsale in 1601 and the final suppression of the rebellion three years later in Ulster, their future existence hung by a precarious thread.

Three years later, in September of 1607 and in what is known as The Flight of the Earls, Hugh O'Neill, 2nd Earl of Tyrone and Rory O'Donnell, 1st Earl of Tyrconnel, sailed into foreign exile from the village of Rathmullan, on the shore of Lough Swilly, in Co. Donegal, accompanied by ninety loyal followers. Cahir O'Doherty had meanwhile been knighted for his military service to the English Crown and appointed admiral of the city of Derry.

In the turbulent politics of the time he was accused of treason and, described as 'that most audacious traitor', he decided to rebel against the policy of plantation by attacking and burning Derry and killing its Crown-appointed governor.

The Crown's vengeance for what is known as O'Doherty's' Rebellion was swift: Cahir O'Doherty was killed and his head lopped off and sent off in triumph for display in Dublin as a dire warning to others.

A number of rebels such as the McLoughlins who had supported O'Doherty were pardoned by James I (James VI of Scotland) in 1609.

But the Flight of the Earls had marked the collapse of the ancient Gaelic order of proud clans such as the McLoughlins, many of whom in succeeding centuries would seek a new life far from Ireland's shores.

One enduring legacy of the McLoughlins comes in the form of one of Ireland's greatest treasures.

Held in the National Museum of Ireland, in Dublin, this is the Bell Shrine of St. Patrick.

During their missionary work throughout the island the saint and his followers used consecrated hand bells, made of iron and quadrangular in shape.

The most precious of these bells was the one used by St. Patrick himself, and known as the Bethechon, or Bell of St. Patrick – believed to have been reverently excavated from his grave in 552 A.D. about sixty years after his death.

Miraculous powers were ascribed to the bell and it was Donnall O'Loghlin, or McLoughlin, Ard Rí of Ireland, who at some stage between 1091 and 1105 arranged for it to be encased in a specially commissioned shrine.

Standing at a little under eight inches in height, the beautifully executed and lavishly decorated shrine also bears McLoughlin's inscription.

The O'Mellan, or O Melaghlin family (an alternative form of 'McLoughlin') were hereditary protectors of the bell and shrine, and towards the end of the eighteenth century a man who claimed to be 'the last of his line' transferred it to the care of another family.

The bell and shrine were acquired by the Royal Irish Academy in the nineteenth century, and later housed in the National Museum.

Meanwhile it is perhaps rather ironical that it was Donnall McLoughlin, a descendant of Niall of the Nine Hostages – who kidnapped the future saint when he was a young lad – who was responsible centuries later for preserving a precious relic of the saint.

Chapter four:

On the world stage

Bearers of the McLoughlin name, in all its variety of spellings, have gained international celebrity through a rich variety of pursuits.

Born in 1886 in Tunbridge Wells, in the English county of Kent, **Victor McLoughlin** became better known as the Academy Award-winning actor **Victor McLaglen**, having changed the spelling of his name for ease of pronunciation.

The son of a Church of England bishop, McLaglen and his family moved to South Africa when he was a young boy.

But the comfortable life of a well-respected bishop's son was not for him, and by the age of 14 he had left home to enlist in the British Army.

Stationed for a time with the Life Guards at Windsor Castle, one of the residences in Britain of the Royal Family, he was eventually forced to leave the army when it was discovered he had enlisted underage.

By the age of 18 the restless McLaglen was in Canada, making a name for himself as a wrestler and heavyweight boxer, at one time taking part in a six-round exhibition bout with famed World Heavyweight boxing champion Jack Johnson.

McLaglen also toured with a circus, offering $25 to anyone who could manage to survive three rounds with him.

By the outbreak of the First World War in 1914, the future film star was back in Britain – this time in the ranks of the 10th Battalion, Middlesex Regiment.

At the end of the war in 1918 he was serving as Military Provost Marshall for the city of Baghdad and by this time had taken the title of Heavyweight Champion of the British Army.

But a future beyond the army and boxing beckoned when McLaglen began to be offered roles in silent films of the time.

His reputation as an actor steadily grew and the 1920s saw him in Hollywood, where he became an established character actor famed for his ability to take on the role of a brawling drunk.

In 1935 he won an Academy Award for Best Actor for his role in *The Informer*, while in 1952 he was nominated for Best Supporting Actor for his memorable role in *The Quiet Man*, that also starred John Wayne and Maureen O'Hara.

America became McLaglen's home, having become a naturalised American citizen, and it was here that he died in 1959.

Still in the world of film **Tom McLoughlin**, born in 1950, is the American film and television director and screenwriter who wrote and directed *Friday the 13th Part VI: Jason Lives*, while **Bronco McLoughlin** is a noted actor, stuntman, and animal trainer.

Irish-born McLoughlin has a Hollywood career that spans more than 30 years, and one of his most memorable and dangerous stunts involved being tied to a wooden cross over the top of a waterfall in the movie *The Mission*, starring Robert De Niro and Jeremy Irons.

Inducted into the Stuntmen's Hall of Fame, he has also appeared in a number of James Bond movies.

From the world of film to the printed word **Robert E. McLaughlin**, born in Chicago in 1908 and who died in 1970, was a distinguished editor at TIME magazine between 1948 and 1969 and also the author of a number of short stories and novels.

Denis McLoughlin, born in 1918 in Bolton, Lancashire, was a prolific illustrator of book jackets, particularly for detective novels, in addition to a range of popular British comic books. He died in 2000.

In contemporary music **Eamon McLoughlin** is the English-born bluegrass musician who plays with the four-piece band The Greencards, formed in Texas in 2003, while **John McLaughlin**, born in 1942 in Doncaster, Yorkshire, is the celebrated British jazz fusion guitarist also known as Mahavishnu John McLaughlin.

McLoughlins have also excelled in the highly competitive world of sport, not least **Maurice McLoughlin**, the American tennis player who was born in 1890.

Known as the California Comet and feared by other tennis players for his powerful serve and overhead volley, he won the singles twice in the U.S. Championships (1912 and 1913), and the doubles on three occasions with fellow player Thomas Bundy.

In 1913 he became the first American to reach the finals of the men's singles at Wimbledon, while a year later he was rated as the number one player in the world.

He was inducted into the International Tennis Hall of Fame in 1957, the year of his death.

Born in 1885 **Jamie McLoughlin** was the American rower who took the silver medal in the double sculls at the 1904 Summer Olympics in St. Louis.

In the world of European football **Alan McLoughlin**, born in 1967 in Manchester of Irish parentage, is the former midfielder and coach of the Republic of Ireland team and who was capped 42 times for his country.

Coleen McLoughlin, born in 1986 in Liverpool, is the much photographed celebrity fiancée of Manchester United and England national team star footballer Wayne Rooney.

In the often cut-throat world of politics **Audrey McLaughlin**, born in 1936 in Dutton, Ontario, was leader of Canada's New Democratic Party from 1989 to 1995, making her the first female leader of a major Canadian federal party.

Born in 1871 near Oshawa, Ontario, **Samuel McLaughlin** was the leading Canadian businessman and philanthropist who founded the McLaughlin Motor Car

Company, one of Canada's first major motorcar manufacturers, in 1907.

Appointed a Companion of the Order of Canada in 1967, he died in 1972.

Born in Drogheda in 1869 **Thomas McLoughlin** was the visionary Irish engineer who successfully campaigned for using the River Shannon as a basis for a hydroelectric and electrification scheme. He died in 1971.

Honoured to this day as 'The Father of Oregon', **Dr. John McLoughlin** was born in 1784 in Rivière-du-Loup, Quebec, of Irish and French-Canadian descent. Qualifying as a medical doctor in 1803 he was appointed as a physician to the fur-gathering post of Fort William, Ontario (now Thunder Bay), later becoming a trader himself.

McLoughlin also identified himself with the rights of the native North Americans while his wife, Marguerite, was the daughter of a native North American woman.

In 1818 he stood trial for the murder of the governor of the Red River colony but was acquitted – and there is evidence to suggest that he may have willingly stood trial in proxy for some native North Americans who had been blamed.

By 1824 he had been appointed by the Hudson's Bay Company as chief factor for the vast Columbia District, also then known by America as Oregon Country, and a year later he built Fort Vancouver (now Vancouver), Washington, as his headquarters.

Despite initial opposition from the Hudson's Bay Company he provided aid in the form of food and other essential supplies to the increasing waves of American settlers to the area.

McLoughlin retired from the Hudson's Bay Company in 1846 and settled with his family in Oregon City, in the Willamette Valley, running a store that was known as 'the last stop on the Oregon Trail.'

The area by this time had become official United States territory, under the terms of the Oregon Treaty, and McLoughlin became a U.S. citizen in 1849, serving as mayor of Oregon City in 1851, six years before his death in 1857.

A bronze statue of McLoughlin was donated by the state of Oregon to America's National Statuary Hall collection in 1953, while in 1957 the Oregon Legislative Assembly officially bestowed on him the title 'Father of Oregon.'

Originally known as Mount Pitt, a stratovolcano in the Cascade Range in southern Oregon is now named **Mount McLoughlin** in his honour.

McLoughlins and their namesakes the McLaughlins have also excelled in defence of their nations' freedoms on the battlefield – whether that is the conventional battlefield or the battlefield of the war against international terrorism.

Born in 1928 in Leeds, Alabama, **Alfred L. McLaughlin** was awarded the Medal of Honor for his heroism during the Korean conflict, decorated by American

President Dwight D. Eisenhower in October of 1953.

McLaughlin, who was later promoted from Private First Class with the 3rd Battalion, 5th Marines, to Master Sergeant, had fought off no less than 200 of the enemy by single-handedly manning two machine guns. He died in 1977.

In more contemporary times **John McLoughlin**, born in 1953, was one of the heroes in the aftermath of the 9/11 terrorist attack on New York's World Trade Center in 2001.

McLoughlin had led a team of four officers from New York's Port Authority police between the two towers on the main concourse in search of survivors, when the South Tower collapsed.

The officers had run towards a freight elevator but were trapped when the concourse itself collapsed.

Two officers died, but McLoughlin and fellow officer William Jimeno were rescued after two former U.S. Marines heard their faint cries for help.

It took twelve hours for Jimeno to be pulled from the rubble, while it took 22 agonising hours to free McLoughlin.

Both men were severely injured but were able to proudly receive the Port Authority's Medal of Honor in June of 2002.

Key dates in Ireland's history from the first settlers to the formation of the Irish Republic:

circa 7000 B.C.	Arrival and settlement of Stone Age people.
circa 3000 B.C.	Arrival of settlers of New Stone Age period.
circa 600 B.C.	First arrival of the Celts.
200 A.D.	Establishment of Hill of Tara, Co. Meath, as seat of the High Kings.
circa 432 A.D.	Christian mission of St. Patrick.
800-920 A.D.	Invasion and subsequent settlement of Vikings.
1002 A.D.	Brian Boru recognised as High King.
1014	Brian Boru killed at battle of Clontarf.
1169-1170	Cambro-Norman invasion of the island.
1171	Henry II claims Ireland for the English Crown.
1366	Statutes of Kilkenny ban marriage between native Irish and English.
1529-1536	England's Henry VIII embarks on religious Reformation.
1536	Earl of Kildare rebels against the Crown.
1541	Henry VIII declared King of Ireland.
1558	Accession to English throne of Elizabeth I.
1565	Battle of Affane.
1569-1573	First Desmond Rebellion.
1579-1583	Second Desmond Rebellion.
1594-1603	Nine Years War.
1606	Plantation' of Scottish and English settlers.
1607	Flight of the Earls.
1632-1636	Annals of the Four Masters compiled.
1641	Rebellion over policy of plantation and other grievances.
1649	Beginning of Cromwellian conquest.
1688	Flight into exile in France of Catholic Stuart monarch James II as Protestant Prince William of Orange invited to take throne of England along with his wife, Mary.
1689	William and Mary enthroned as joint monarchs; siege of Derry.
1690	Jacobite forces of James defeated by William at battle of the Boyne (July) and Dublin taken.

1691	Athlone taken by William; Jacobite defeats follow at Aughrim, Galway, and Limerick; conflict ends with Treaty of Limerick (October) and Irish officers allowed to leave for France.
1695	Penal laws introduced to restrict rights of Catholics; banishment of Catholic clergy.
1704	Laws introduced constricting rights of Catholics in landholding and public office.
1728	Franchise removed from Catholics.
1791	Foundation of United Irishmen republican movement.
1796	French invasion force lands in Bantry Bay.
1798	Defeat of Rising in Wexford and death of United Irishmen leaders Wolfe Tone and Lord Edward Fitzgerald.
1800	Act of Union between England and Ireland.
1803	Dublin Rising under Robert Emmet.
1829	Catholics allowed to sit in Parliament.
1845-1849	The Great Hunger: thousands starve to death as potato crop fails and thousands more emigrate.
1856	Phoenix Society founded.
1858	Irish Republican Brotherhood established.
1873	Foundation of Home Rule League.
1893	Foundation of Gaelic League.
1904	Foundation of Irish Reform Association.
1913	Dublin strikes and lockout.
1916	Easter Rising in Dublin and proclamation of an Irish Republic.
1917	Irish Parliament formed after Sinn Fein election victory.
1919-1921	War between Irish Republican Army and British Army.
1922	Irish Free State founded, while six northern counties remain part of United Kingdom as Northern Ireland, or Ulster; civil war up until 1923 between rival republican groups.
1949	Foundation of Irish Republic after all remaining constitutional links with Britain are severed.